HOCKEY

COLORING BOOK

BLUE WAVE PRESS

HOCKEY

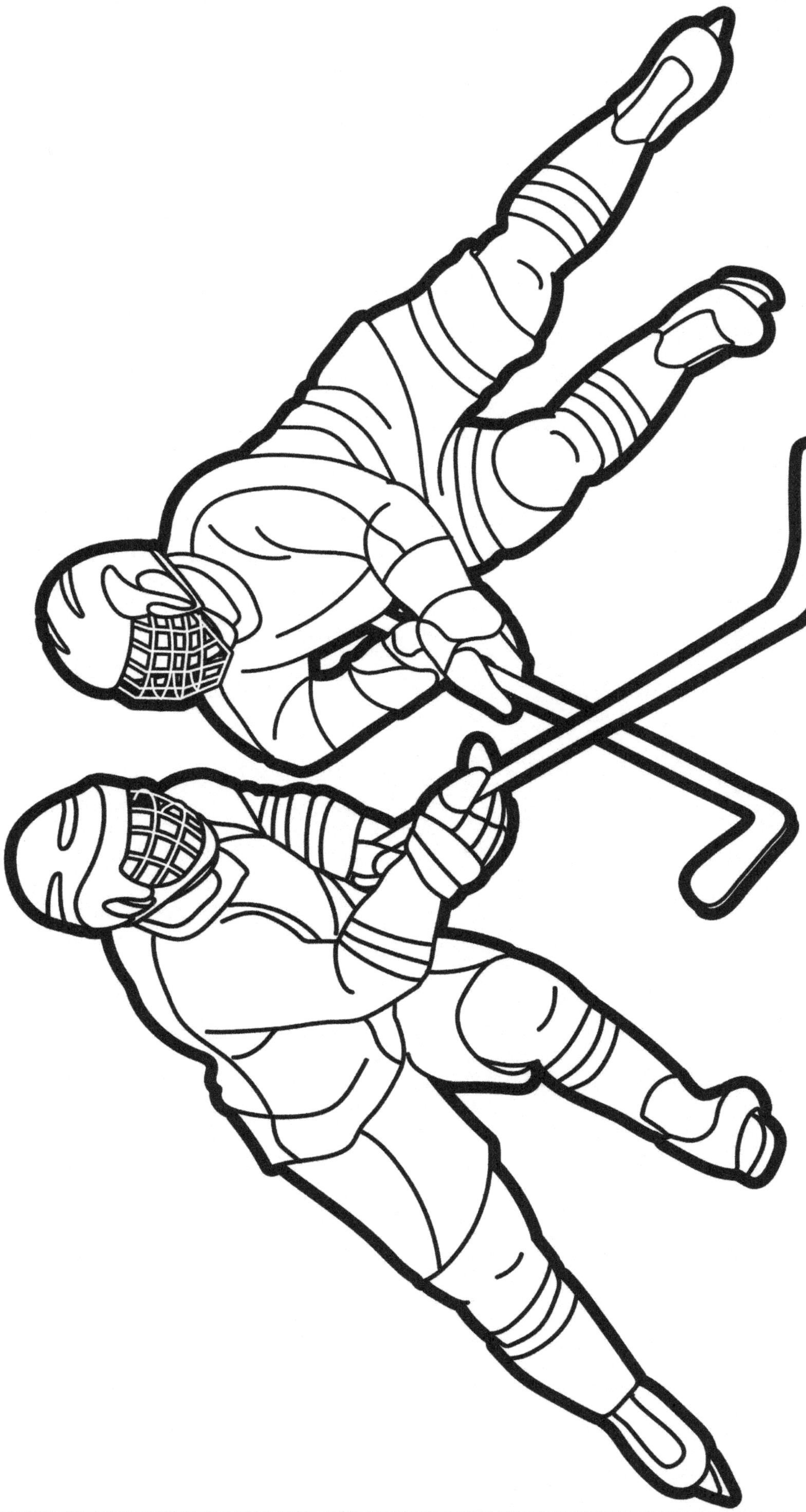

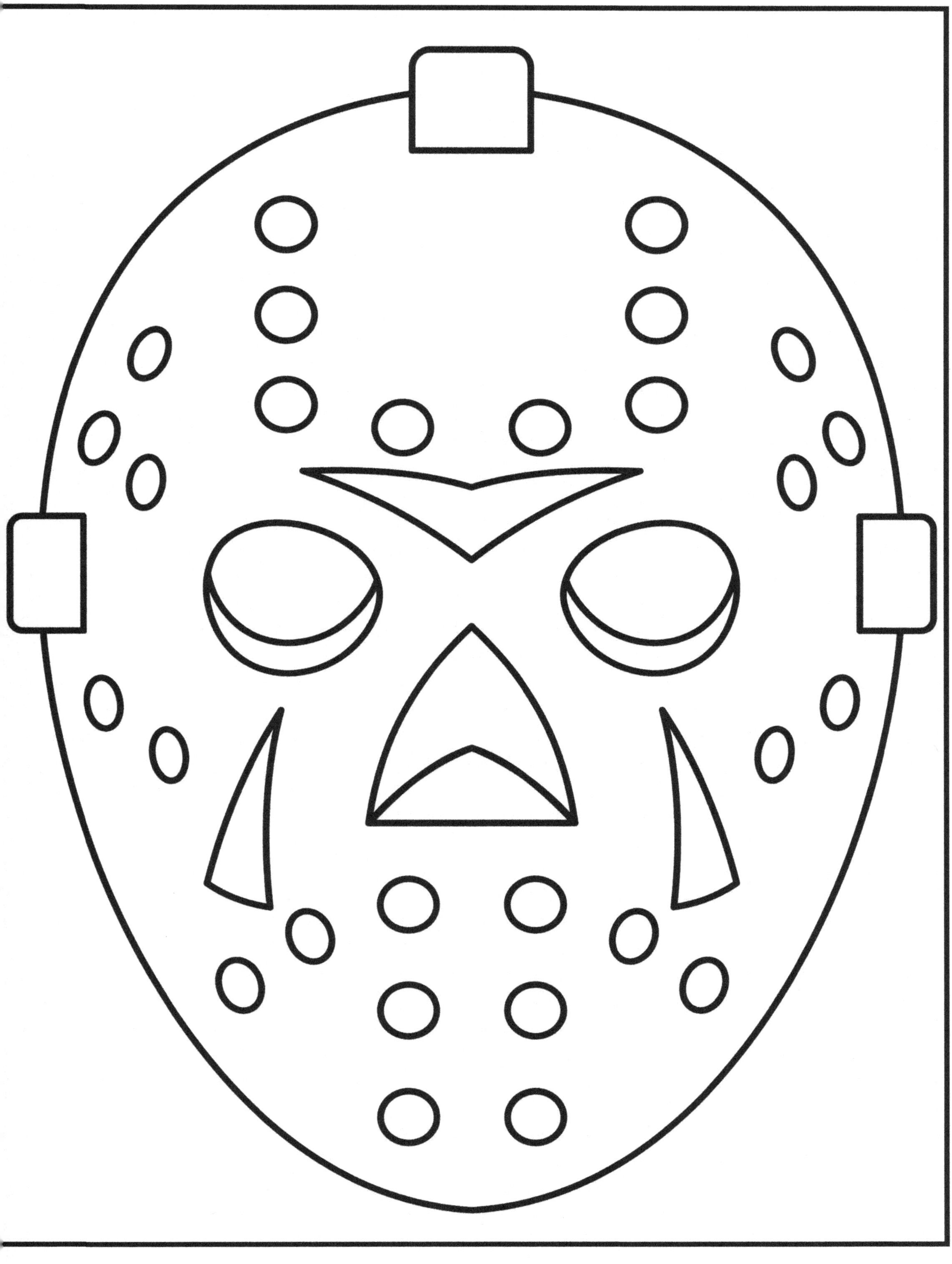

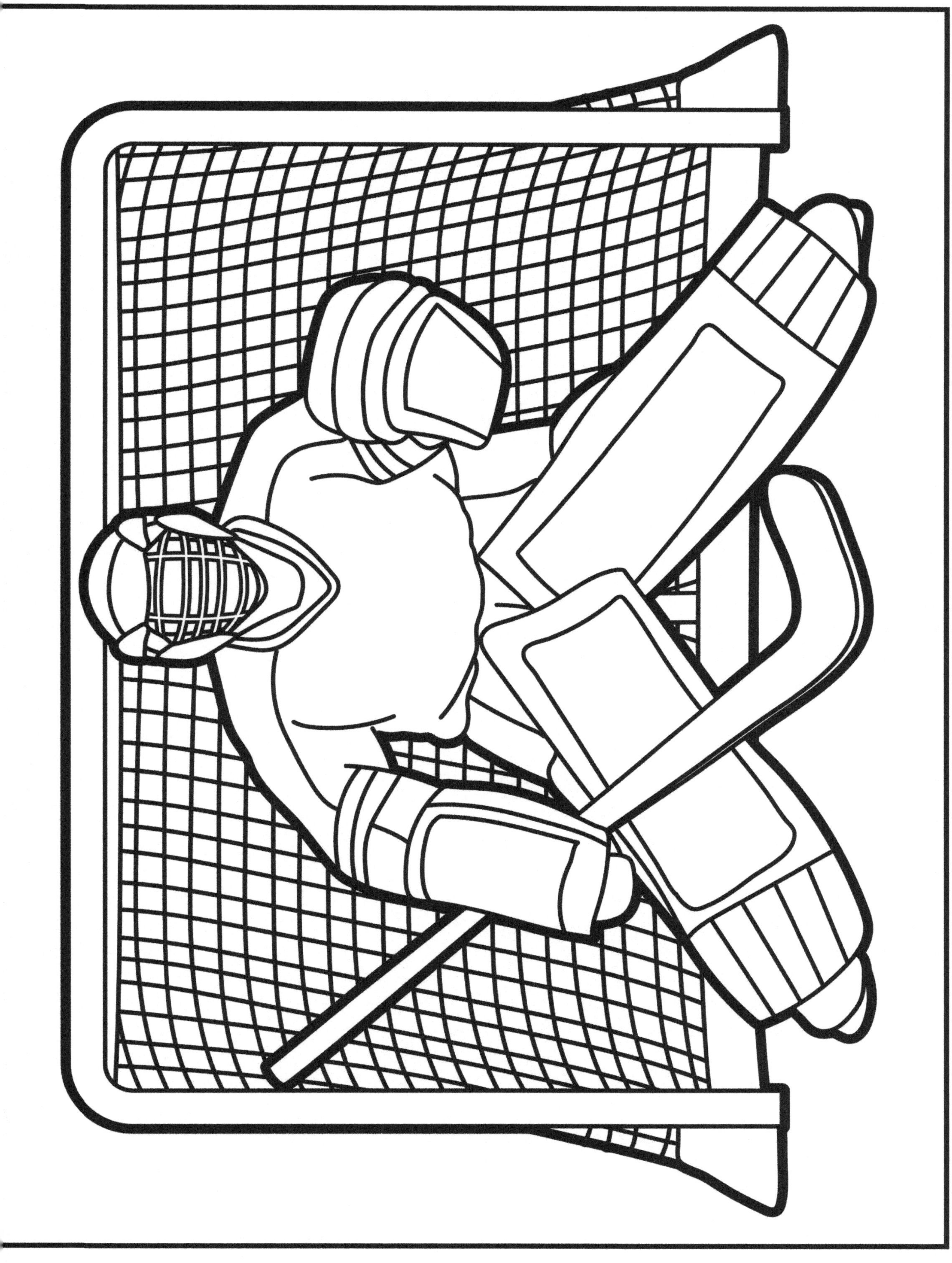

10

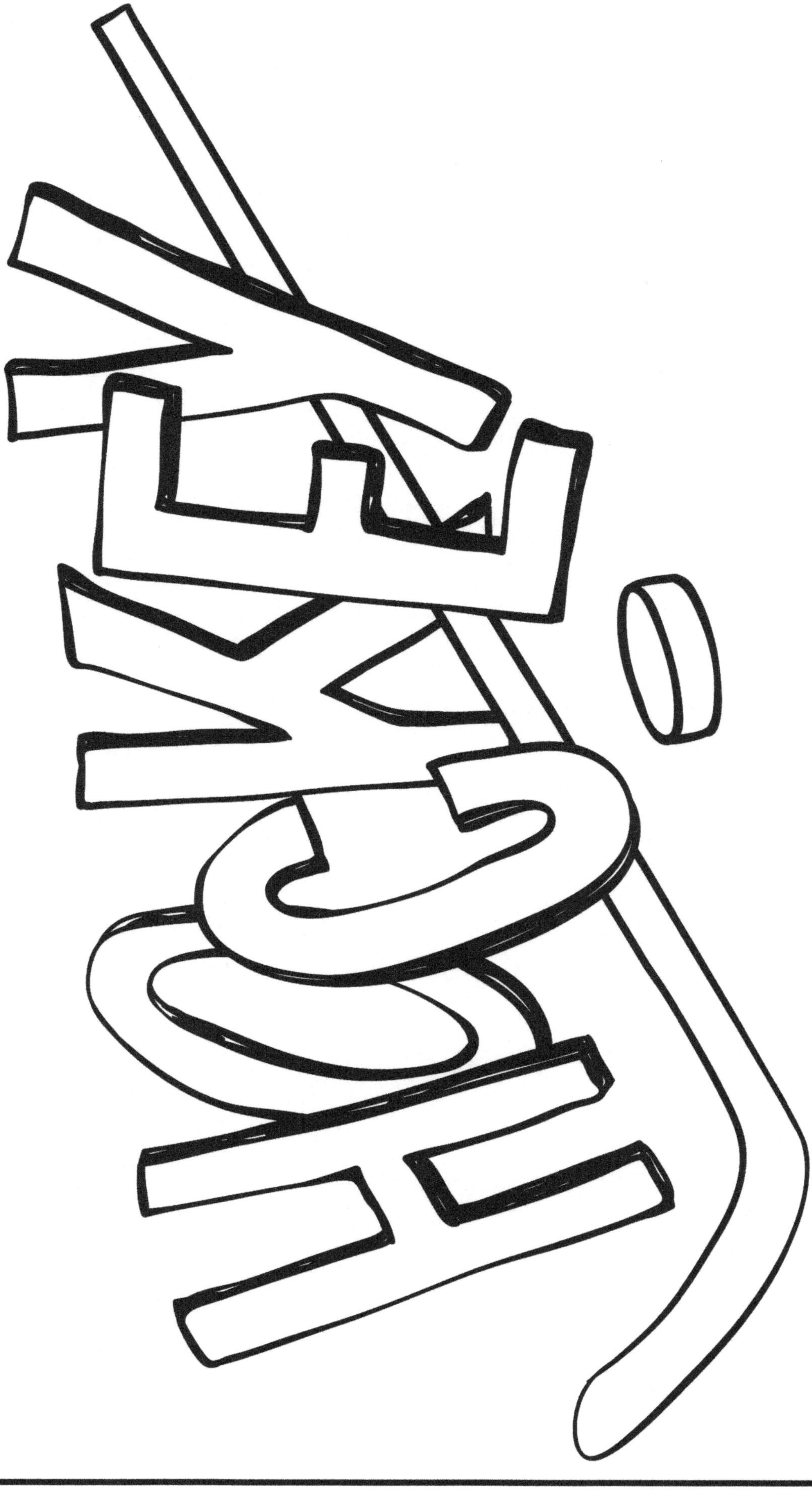
HOCKEY

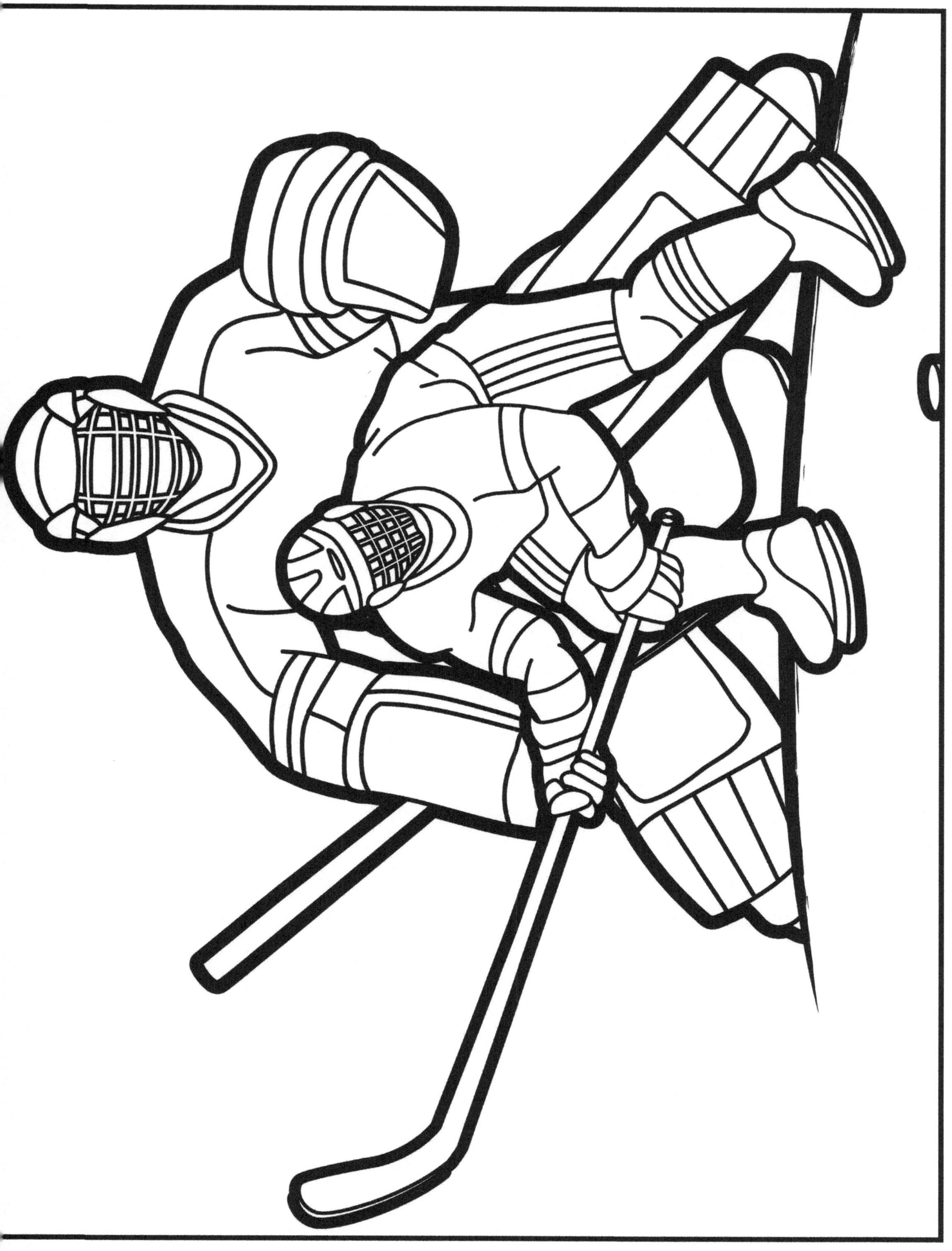

A
23

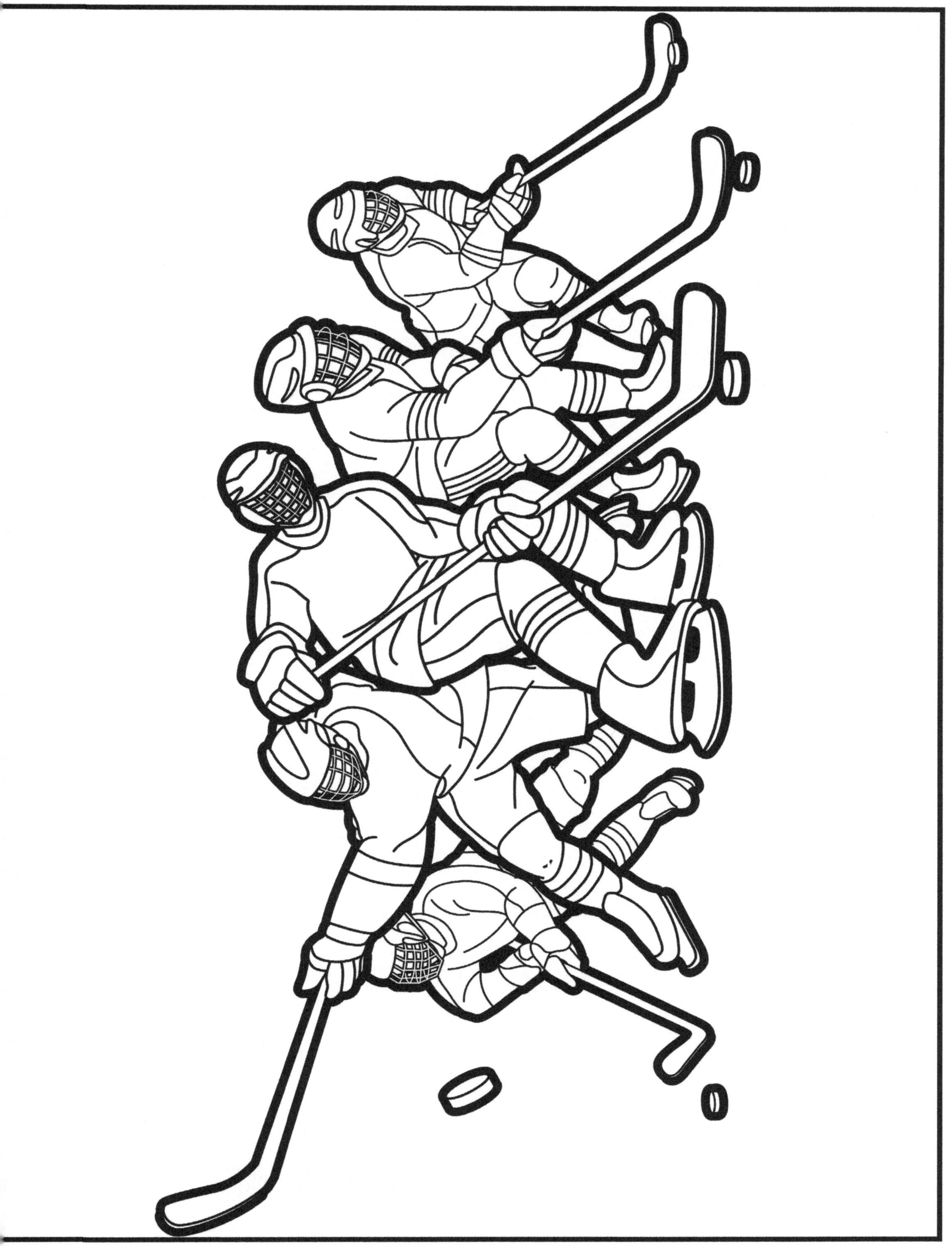

Made in the USA
Monee, IL
18 November 2021

82456760R00039